INSIDE THE AIRPORT

Written by Mark Davies • *Illustrated by Rick Geary*

A CALICO BOOK
Published by Contemporary Books, Inc.
CHICAGO • NEW YORK

Library of Congress Cataloging-in-Publication Data
Davies, Mark, 1963–
Inside the airport / Mark Davies ; illustrations by Rick Geary.
p.   cm.
Summary: Todd receives a tour of the airport and discovers how its
many operations work.
ISBN 0-8092-4274-5
1. Airports—Juvenile literature.   [1. Airports.]   I.Geary,
Rick, ill.   II. Title.
TL725.D38   1989
387.7'36—dc20   89-34926
                                                              CIP
                                                              AC

Published by Contemporary Books, Inc.
180 North Michigan Avenue, Chicago, Illinois 60601
Manufactured in the United States of America
Library of Congress Catalog Card Number: 89-34926
International Standard Book Number: 0-8092-4274-5

Published simultaneously in Canada by Beaverbooks, Ltd.
195 Allstate Parkway, Valleywood Business Park
Markham, Ontario L3R 4T8 Canada

We're here, we're here!" shouted Todd when he saw the big sign that said FLYAWAY INTERNATIONAL AIRPORT. Todd's dog, Scamp, wagged his tail as though he knew something special was happening.

It was. Grandma, who lived in London, England, was coming to spend the summer with Todd's family. And Todd and his mother were meeting her at the airport.

Todd had never been to an airport before. "I can't wait!" he kept saying.

3

Todd's mom drove past many signs that told them where the different airlines were located. "There's ours," said Mom.

Parking the car, she said, "It won't take very long to get Grandma. Stick close to me now, so you don't get lost." Todd grabbed his mother's hand and held tight.

Mom was looking at a row of TV screens. "What are those for?" asked Todd.

"They tell what time the planes are leaving and arriving," Mom replied. "They are now telling us that Grandma's plane is late. Let's go to the information counter and find out what happened."

Inside the airport building lots of people were going in all different directions. "Wow!" Todd said as he looked around. Scamp seemed interested, too.

At the information counter was Pam, an old friend of Todd's mom. Pam explained that Grandma's plane had taken off late.

"I'm sorry," Pam told them, "but the flight from London won't be here for another two hours." Seeing Todd's disappointed face, she said, "I'm off duty now. Why don't I give Todd a tour of the airport while you're waiting?"

"Oh boy!" said Todd. "Can Scamp come, too?" Pam smiled but shook her head. Dogs were not allowed any farther into the airport.

"That's OK," said Todd's mom. "I've got some errands to run, and I'll take Scamp with me. Then I'll meet you and Pam in two hours."

As Pam and Todd started off into the crowd, Todd felt just like an explorer in a new world!

6

First, Pam took Todd up some stairs to get a good view of the building. "Flyaway Airport is one of the biggest airports in the world," she said proudly. "It's like a small city, with its own restaurants, banks, and shops. More than fourteen thousand people work here, keeping it clean and in working order. Flyaway is an international airport. That means planes from all over the world stop here when they arrive in the United States."

"We're in the main building of the airport now," Pam told Todd. "It's called the passenger terminal. Eighty thousand passengers go through this airport each day."

"Eighty thousand!" said Todd, giving a low whistle. "There aren't that many people living in my town!"

"Let's pretend you're a passenger going on a trip," said Pam. "I'll show you what happens from the time you get to the airport until the time you leave."

"The first thing a passenger does when he or she gets to Flyaway is come to a ticket counter," said Pam. "This is where you get your ticket and check your bags."

Todd watched the passengers' suitcases disappear through a small door. "Where do all the bags go?" he asked.

"They're put on a small moving road called a conveyor belt, which takes them out to the plane," Pam answered. "Later you'll see where they end up."

"Now, to get to your plane, first you have to go through these machines," said Pam.

"What do they do?" asked Todd.

"This one is an x-ray machine," explained Pam. "It can see what's inside your bag when it's closed.

"And this is called a metal detector," she continued. "It helps the airport police stop anyone from carrying something that can be dangerous onto the plane."

So they could explore the large airport more quickly, Pam and Todd got into a special cart. They drove past many big waiting areas where people were sitting, and then they stopped at one. "This is called a gate," Pam said. "Passengers wait here for their planes."

An airplane was sitting on the ground outside the window. A tunnel on wheels moved out between the building and the plane. "The passengers walk through that tunnel to get onto the plane," Pam said. "Do you want to see inside?"

"Oh yes! Please!" Todd exclaimed.

Inside the plane, all sorts of people were busy doing different things. "Planes come and go very fast," she told him. "They have to be ready to fly again very quickly."

"Do I smell food?" Todd asked.

"Yes!" said Pam. "If it's a long plane ride, passengers will get a meal. They may even get to see a movie!"

Pam knocked on a little door toward the front of the plane. Inside was the cockpit, a small room where the pilot sat ready to fly the plane. The walls and ceiling were covered with switches and dials.

"These instruments tell us everything we need to know to fly a plane," said Captain Williams. "For example, they tell us how high the plane is and which direction we're going."

"I'd never know how to fly a plane," Todd said.

"Sure you would!" smiled the captain. "But you'd have to go to school to learn."

"Come on," said Pam. "Captain Williams has lots to do, and so do we." Todd saluted the pilot and wished him a safe and happy journey.

They went back into the tunnel and down
some steps to the ground.

"What are these people doing?" asked Todd.

"Some of them are filling the gas tanks of
the plane," answered Pam. "Guess where the
gas tanks are?"

Todd gave up.

"In the wings!" said Pam.

"Planes must be checked every time they fly," one of the workers told Todd. "We have to make sure everything is working right. We check the wing flaps and tail flaps that move up and down to help the plane get off the ground. We make sure doors are secure and all the bolts are tight. We check everything from the engine to the wheels!"

Then Pam pointed to a small opening in a nearby wall of the airport building. Pop! Out came a suitcase . . . then another . . . and another!

"Remember asking me where the passengers' bags go?" she asked Todd. "Well, they end up out here."

Todd could see workers sorting the bags and then loading them onto carts and driving them to the different planes.

"The people who look after your bags are called baggage handlers," said Pam.

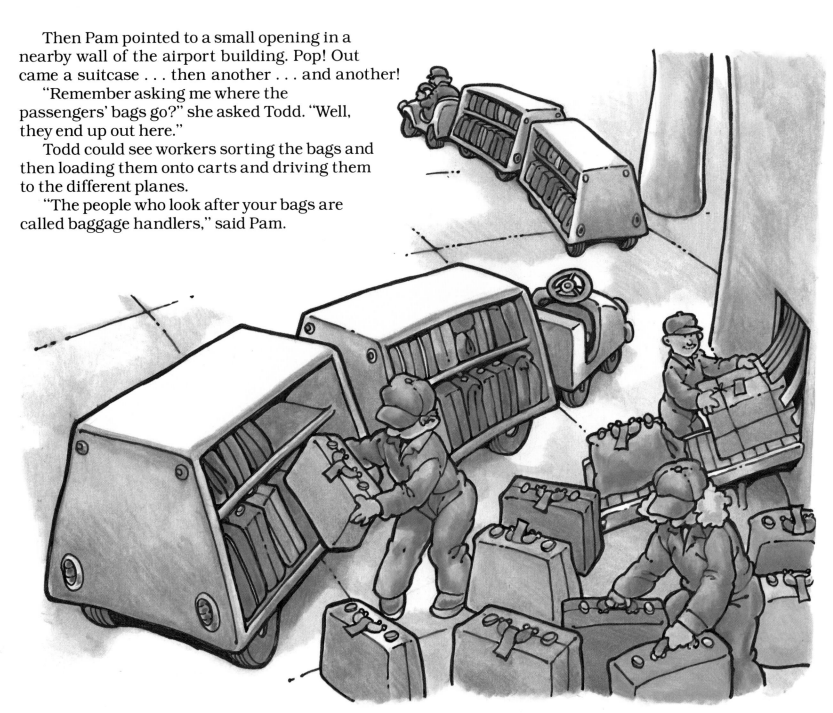

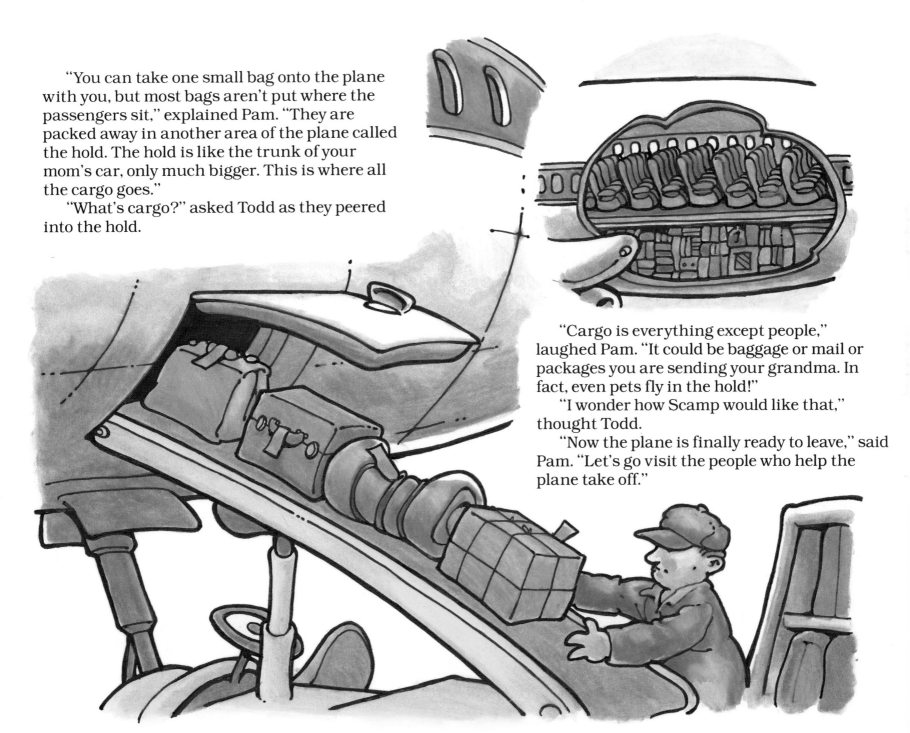

"You can take one small bag onto the plane with you, but most bags aren't put where the passengers sit," explained Pam. "They are packed away in another area of the plane called the hold. The hold is like the trunk of your mom's car, only much bigger. This is where all the cargo goes."

"What's cargo?" asked Todd as they peered into the hold.

"Cargo is everything except people," laughed Pam. "It could be baggage or mail or packages you are sending your grandma. In fact, even pets fly in the hold!"

"I wonder how Scamp would like that," thought Todd.

"Now the plane is finally ready to leave," said Pam. "Let's go visit the people who help the plane take off."

17

Todd and Pam drove to a tall building that
was far away from the passenger terminal.
Todd thought the building looked like an
ice-cream cone.

"This is the control tower," Pam told Todd.
"This is where people tell the planes where to
move around the airport. They need big
windows to see everything. Let's go up!"

Inside, Todd and Pam took an elevator to the top of the control tower.

It was very quiet in the tower except for a few people who were talking into microphones. There were computers, instruments, and machines everywhere. "Quite a view, isn't it, son?" asked Jeff, one of the people who worked there.

"Yes!" Todd said. He could see the whole airport through the windows. The planes on the ground looked tiny, and there were roads going in every direction.

"More than a thousand planes take off and land every day at this airport!" said Jeff. "It's our job to make sure the planes move quickly and don't run into each other. We're called air-traffic controllers.

"There are two types of roads at the airport," explained Jeff. "The two long, straight roads are called runways. All the smaller roads are called taxiways. These are the roads planes use to get from the terminal to the runway."

"Why are the runways so long?" asked Todd.

"Planes go very fast," answered Jeff. "When a big plane is in the air it can be going six hundred miles an hour. So when it lands, it needs a lot of space to slow down. When it takes off, it needs a long road to build up enough speed to get off the ground."

Todd listened to Debra, one of the other controllers, give directions to a plane, "Wingtip 167, taxi into position and hold," Debra said into a microphone.

Jeff pointed to a plane that was moving onto the runway. "That's the plane Debra's talking to," he whispered. "The pilot can hear what she is saying through a radio. She's telling the pilot to move into the right place for takeoff.

"We've got a machine that can see planes at night when it's dark or when they are too far away for you or me to see," said Jeff. He pointed to a green screen with little dots on it. "This is called a radar screen. Its eyes are in that big white ball you saw on the roof. Each dot on the screen is a plane. We can tell where each plane is and how fast and in which direction it's going."

21

Pam took Todd to see some other buildings at the airport.

"The passenger terminal you visited earlier is only part of the airport. There are other terminal buildings, including one for small planes," Pam said. "A lot of people fly just for fun, and this is where they keep their planes. Sometimes a big company will have its own plane so it can fly important people around. The small planes are parked here."

The cargo terminal was their next stop.

"This is where the post office sorts all the letters and packages that are sent around the United States and to other countries," Pam told Todd.

"Nowadays almost anything can fly around the world. We get TVs from Japan, food from Europe, clothes from India—even cars are flown in from other countries in special cargo planes."

"Animals fly, too," said Pam. "A lot of animals come from all over the world for our zoos. Last week we got an elephant from Africa! But you can't just leave animals in boxes—they have to be looked after by an animal doctor. The doctor makes sure all the foreign animals are healthy."

Next, they drove the cart over to a huge building. It was lit up with bright lights inside, and many people were working on one of the big planes.

"This is an airplane garage. It's called a hangar." Pam explained. "Sometimes a plane has to be fixed here before it can fly again."

"This is the only building you haven't seen yet," said Pam. "It's the Airport Services Center. The airport police have their headquarters here. They even have a cell where they can lock up people if they do something wrong."

"Like what?" asked Todd

"Some people try to steal planes," Pam explained. "Others try to bring things into the country that are not allowed.

"We also have a small doctor's office here in case someone becomes ill or gets hurt."

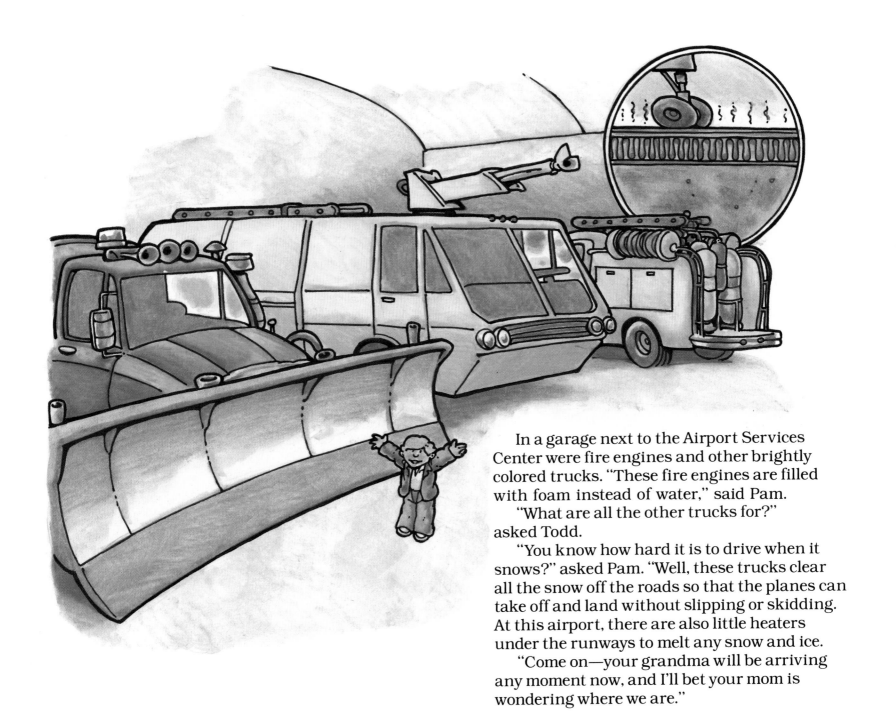

In a garage next to the Airport Services Center were fire engines and other brightly colored trucks. "These fire engines are filled with foam instead of water," said Pam.

"What are all the other trucks for?" asked Todd.

"You know how hard it is to drive when it snows?" asked Pam. "Well, these trucks clear all the snow off the roads so that the planes can take off and land without slipping or skidding. At this airport, there are also little heaters under the runways to melt any snow and ice.

"Come on—your grandma will be arriving any moment now, and I'll bet your mom is wondering where we are."

During the drive back to the main passenger terminal, Todd watched a jumbo jet land. "This is the flight your grandma is on," said Pam. Todd waved at the plane.

A woman with bright orange sticks was waving to the pilot up in the plane. "She's showing the pilot where to park the plane," said Pam.

The plane stopped and the moving tunnel was wheeled out to the plane's door.

28

A team of baggage handlers opened the cargo door and began unloading all the bags onto a small truck right away. "They don't waste any time, do they?" asked Todd.

"No, they don't," laughed Pam. "They want to get all the cargo off as fast as possible so the passengers don't have to wait long for their suitcases."

"Look," said Todd as he pointed to a small window in the plane. He thought he could see Grandma waving. "It's Grandma! It's Grandma!" he shouted. "She's here!"

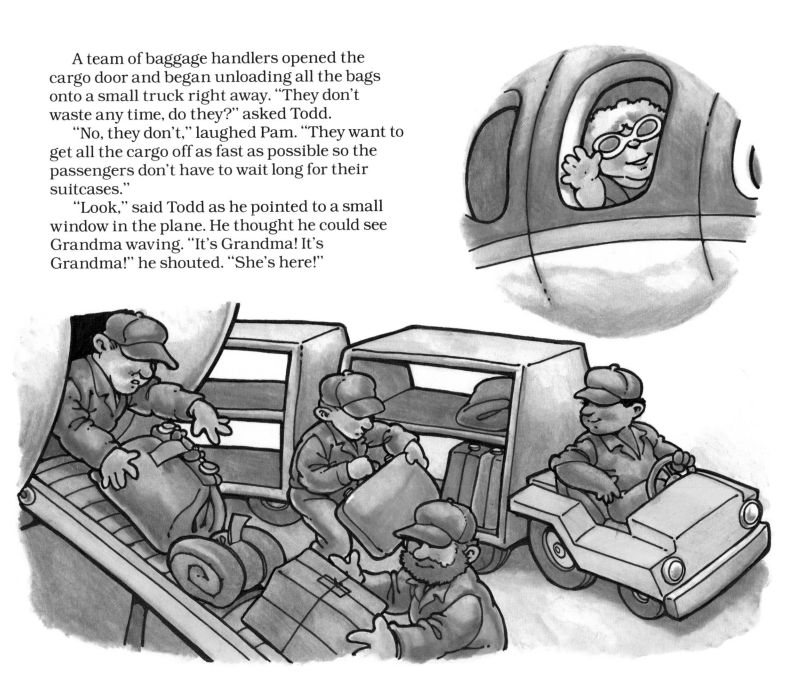

Pam took Todd inside to meet her at the gate.

"Everyone coming from other countries has to have a special pass to visit the United States. It's called a passport," said Pam.

Todd watched as his grandma's passport was checked and as government inspectors checked her bags. Then he ran up and hugged her. "I'm so glad you're finally here, Grandma!" he said. "This is my new friend, Pam!"

Todd was helping Grandma get her bags when Todd's mother arrived. Scamp was waiting in the car.

"I had a great time, Mom," said Todd. "But will I ever get to be a *real* passsenger?"

"Maybe you can go visit Grandma in England someday," Mom answered. Grandma and Todd both thought that was a fine idea.

Grandma, Mom, and Todd were ready to go home. "Thanks, Pam!" said Todd as he waved good-bye. "I'll never forget my trip inside the airport."